W9-CPP-532

Ready, Set, Cheer!

CHEERLEADING STUNTS AND TUMBLING

LISA MULLARKEY

Enslow Publishers, Inc.

40 Industrial Road
Box 398
Berkeley Heights, NJ 07922
USA

http://www.enslow.com

*Many thanks to Emily Beggiato, Erika Lipinski, Alyssa Materazzo,
Abby Michta, Sarah Mullarkey, and Bryanna Papcun
for their contributions to this book. Special thanks to Steven DeCasperis for
several of the photos used here.*

Library of Congress Cataloging-in-Publication Data

Mullarkey, Lisa.
    Cheerleading stunts and tumbling / Lisa Mullarkey.
    p. cm. — (Ready, set, cheer!)
    Includes index.
    Summary: "Readers will find out about the differences between tumbling and stunting, and
learn basic moves in both"—Provided by publisher.
    ISBN 978-0-7660-3537-9
    1. Cheerleading—Juvenile literature. 2. Acrobatics—Juvenile literature. 3.
Tumbling—Juvenile literature. I. Title.
    LB3635.M855 2010   791.6'4—dc22
    2010003872

ISBN-13: 978-1-59845-200-6 (paperback)

Printed in the United States of America
062010 Lake Book Manufacturing, Inc., Melrose Park, IL

10 9 8 7 6 5 4 3 2 1

To Our Readers: We have done our best to make sure all Internet addresses in this book were active
and appropriate when we went to press. However, the author and the publisher have no control over
and assume no liability for the material available on those Internet sites or on other Web sites they
may link to. Any comments or suggestions can be sent by e-mail to comments@enslow.com or to the
address on the back cover.

♻ Enslow Publishers, Inc., is committed to printing our books on recycled paper. The paper in every
book contains 10% to 30% post-consumer waste (PCW). The cover board on the outside of each book
contains 100% PCW. Our goal is to do our part to help young people and the environment too!

Illustration Credits: Associated Press, pp. 4, 10; © Tom Carter/Alamy, pp. 7, 21; Steven DeCasperis,
pp. 6, 26, 30, 44; Nicole diMella/Enslow Publishers, Inc., pp. 9, 20, 24, 35, 36–37, 40–41, 45; Ray
Moller, © Dorling Kindersley, p. 38; Getty Images, pp. 27, 28; Jeff Haynes/Reuters/Landov, p. 16;
Iconica/Getty Images, p. 13; Index Stock Imagery/Photolibrary, p. 31; Shelly Lennon/Ai Wire/Landov,
p. 47; Punchstock, p. 42; Shutterstock.com, pp. 34, 39; Taxi/Getty Images, p. 25; © Friedman Wagner-
Dobler/iStockphoto.com, p. 18.

Cover Illustration: © George Shelley/CORBIS.

CONTENTS

A cheerleader flies through the air into the arms of her teammates below.

1 PERFORM WITH POWER

Do you remember the first time you saw a cheerleader fly through the air? Pose on one foot at the top of a perfect pyramid? Perform a running back handspring? Did your jaw drop? Your stomach flinch? Cheerleaders use stunts and tumbles to electrify crowds.

If your cheer squad wants to add pizzazz to its performances, take its routine to the next level, and get a leg up on the competition, adding stunts and tumbling will do the trick! The more stunting and tumbling your squad does, the louder the "oohs" and "aahs" in the stands.

Tumbling is the act of turning your body end over end like a cartwheel. *Stunting* uses mounts, pyramids, and tosses. Put them together, and you have a dynamic, powerful routine!

It takes a long time to perfect stunting and tumbling.

It's thrilling to see a cheerleader posed on one foot high in the air.

You must have adult supervision and spotters while learning them. With lots of practice and a helpful coach, you will soon fly through the air with confidence!

Cheerleaders who stunt and tumble are good athletes. Are you in good shape? Most gymnasts and cheerleaders are good stunters and tumblers, because their bodies are flexible. They are in tip-top condition. As tumbling has become more popular in cheer routines, more gymnasts are becoming cheerleaders.

A Balancing Act

Successful stunting takes teamwork. All stunts have three positions: *flyer, base,* and *spotter.*

Flyers are the cheerleaders at the top of the stunt. They are like acrobats. They fly through the air. They make it look easy. Their moves need to be sharp. They must remember to keep their arms and legs close to their bodies. Flyers need to keep their balance while on the bases. The best way to do this is to not let their feet go more than shoulder-width apart. Sometimes a flyer has to support her weight on her hands when lifting off the bases. So, a flyer must have strong muscles!

High school cheerleaders in Maryland perform. The flyer is the one at the top of the stunt.

Do you want to be a flyer? Do you have what it takes? You must have …

- ★ *confidence and trust!* Flying through the air can be scary. Are you confident that the bases will catch you? You must trust your teammates and your coach.

- ★ *nerves of steel!* You cannot be scared of heights. A flyer is tossed up high in the air to perform the stunts.

- ★ *good eye contact and a smile plastered on your face!* That is hard to have when you are tossed high in the air!

TIP: Flyers must know how to fall correctly into the arms of bases. Practice falling by starting off on a low chair. Have your bases stand behind the chair. As you fall, they will catch you the correct way. It takes practice. When you feel comfortable with the bases and spotters, you are ready to move into your stunts.

Bases are at the bottom of the stunt. They are the foundation. They are the glue that keeps the stunt together. You cannot have a flyer without a base. Bases must be strong. They must lift and throw flyers through the air. Bases must have good concentration skills. They must focus on catching the flyer. It is important that they use their arms and legs to lift the flyer. They should not use their back muscles. It will hurt their backs. They cannot shy away from the flyer when the flyer lands—no flinching or jumping back allowed.

Bases form the foundation of the stunt.

Do you want to be a base? Do you have what it takes? You must have …

★ *confidence!* You need to be confident of your strength and catching abilities.

★ *patience!* Patience with the flyer and with other bases is a must! It takes a lot of practice to get the stunt correct. You must understand that practice makes perfect.

★ *muscles!* Strong arms and leg muscles are necessary! You need to exercise and strengthen your muscles. The safety of the flyer depends on it.

University of Nebraska cheerleaders do a stunt. The spotters ensure the flyer's safety by focusing on her at all times.

Spotters are the ones who make sure the flyer stays safe. They surround the bases and flyer. Spotters must pay attention to the flyer at all times. They must never take their eyes off of the flyer, because one roaming eye could result in severe injury.

Spotters must be quick thinkers. If a flyer is about to fall, a spotter moves in to help catch her. The more difficult the stunt is, the more spotters that are needed. Spotters' hands should be touching the flyer or their arms should be up toward the flyer.

Do you want to be a spotter? Do you have what it takes? You must have …

★ *perfect timing!* You need to stay close to the flyer and be ready to step in and catch the flyer no matter what way she falls.

★ *a very strong attention span.* You cannot take your eyes off of the flyer—not even for a minute! No waving to the crowds. Forget about searching for a friend in the stands. You are there for the flyer at all times.

★ *an understanding* that your number-one job is to keep the flyer safe. Protect her neck and head at all times.

Roll With It

Many cheerleaders want to be flyers. Why? Because they are at the center of attention. But not everyone can be a flyer. In fact, cheerleaders do not get to pick which positions they

SAFETY RULES

Cheerleaders must work together to make sure the stunt is safe. Here are some important rules that everyone must follow when stunting:

1. **During a stunt, only the back spotter talks. By having only one person speak, the group will stay focused.**

2. **Every stunt is timed perfectly. The back spotter will call out counts.**

3. **Everyone must give 100 percent effort at all times. The flyer's safety depends on it.**

4. **Make sure there is adequate space for stunting. Check the ceiling level and make sure your area is clear of obstacles.**

5. **Have plenty of soft surfaces to land on: grass or mats. Some stunts are only allowed to be performed on a mat. Your coach must approve all elements of a stunt.**

want. The coach does. She will work with all the cheerleaders to find out their strengths and weaknesses. Your coach wants your team to be the best it can be while keeping everyone safe. She takes a long time to fill each stunt position. Why? Because she wants to make sure it is a *safe* stunt team.

According to Carol Whitmore, a twelve-year coaching veteran, picking positions is a tough decision. "You need to take each cheerleader's strengths into consideration. Sometimes, the end result is not what the individual is happy

"IF YOU DON'T LEAP, YOU'LL NEVER KNOW WHAT IT'S LIKE TO FLY."

GUY FINLEY

with, but it is what is best for the team. A quote I often use is that there is no 'I' in team."

So does this mean that once a base or spotter, always a base or spotter? Nope! "Some switching usually needs to happen," says Whitmore, "whether it is due to an injury or, most often, for the safety of the team." She adds, "It helps if each girl is properly trained on more than one position. A good coach trains cheerleaders in various positions."

2

BUILDING BLOCKS FOR SAVVY STUNTING

Cheerleaders perform beginner and advanced stunts. No matter what type your squad does, all stunters need to master the basics. You must learn the building blocks. Those building blocks apply to all levels of stunts.

Count It Out

Cheerleaders use counts to coordinate stunts for flyers, bases, and spotters. It is safer than everyone trying to talk to each other throughout a stunt. In cheerleading, most counts are in eights. You must know what you are supposed to be doing on each count. The back spotter leads the counts. Everyone's timing needs to be perfect. If the bases are supposed to bend on "three," all bases had *better* bend on three. Imagine if one base bends but the other throws the flyer in the air. The results could be disastrous. That is why stunts are practiced

Kent State cheerleaders at a basketball game. For stunts that thrill fans, timing is crucial.

dozens of times with the counts. They are practiced so much that you will be able to visualize each movement/count in your head.

Get a Grip

All stunts require team members to hold on to each other, and each stunt requires them to hold on in a certain way. These holds are called *grips*. Grips are important for safety. By using the correct grip for each stunt, you are helping to keep the flyer safe. She will not fall or slip. Grips make the stunts look better, too. If everyone used a different grip, it would look sloppy and could be dangerous.

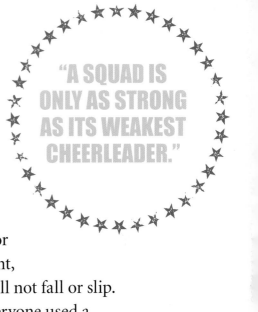

"A SQUAD IS ONLY AS STRONG AS ITS WEAKEST CHEERLEADER."

★ *Handshake grip:* The flyer and base interlock hands as if they were shaking hands. This is used for shoulder sits, chair mounts, and basic dismounts.

★ *Extension prep grip:* The base grabs the heel and toe of the flyer and holds her at chest level. The back spotter holds the flyer at the waist. If the stunt goes higher, the back spotter must hold on to the ankles.

★ *Four fingers forward grip:* The base supports the flyer under the arm with one hand. The fingers are forward facing the crowd.

★ *Thigh stand grip:* The base's arm is wrapped around the flyer's thigh with the hand in a fist. The outside hand goes under the flyer's toe for support.

If an extension prep grip goes high enough, the back spotter holds on to the flyer's ankles.

What Goes Up Must Come Down: Dismounts

Dismounts are an important part of stunting. A dismount is how the flyer gets back on, or returns to, the ground. The counts for most dismounts are "one, two, down, up." It's when the spotter says "up" that the bases "pop" the flyer up into the air and catch her.

There are several types of dismounts. Some dismounts are spectacular to watch! However, all beginners must start with basic dismounts. Master these before moving on to more difficult ones.

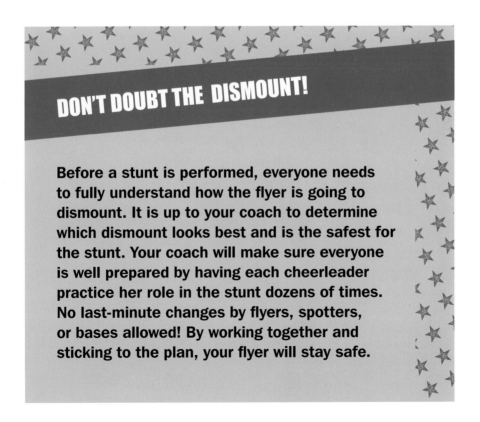

DON'T DOUBT THE DISMOUNT!

Before a stunt is performed, everyone needs to fully understand how the flyer is going to dismount. It is up to your coach to determine which dismount looks best and is the safest for the stunt. Your coach will make sure everyone is well prepared by having each cheerleader practice her role in the stunt dozens of times. No last-minute changes by flyers, spotters, or bases allowed! By working together and sticking to the plan, your flyer will stay safe.

This flyer is preparing to dismount by holding the hands of the front spotter.

The easiest dismount is the *step off.* In this dismount, the flyer holds the hands of each base and simply steps off onto the ground. The flyer gives most of her weight to the bases. She bends her knees to make a softer landing. The spotter in the back will hold on to the flyer's waist until the flyer lands safely. The spotter will call out the counts for everyone.

A *cradle* dismount is exciting to watch! It is much more difficult to do. The flyer is popped into the air. The bases catch her as she lands in a sitting position with her feet straight out. The

In a cradle dismount, the flyer lands in the bases' arms with her legs out straight.

flyer wraps her arms around her bases' necks as she lands. Usually, two spotters are used. The back spotter calls out the counts and holds on to the flyer's ankles at the beginning of the stunt. The front spotter will support the flyer's feet in the cradle when she lands. This dismount takes a lot of practice.

A *pencil drop* dismount is easy and fun. The bases push the flyer's legs together and then drop their arms. The flyer's legs and arms are locked tight. Her arms are above her head. As the flyer comes down, the bases bear-hug her waist to help guide her to the ground.

3 STUNTS: BRING 'EM ON!

There are two kinds of stunts. *Partner stunts* involve one partner. *Mounts,* or *pyramids,* involve three or more people. Both types are fun to do! Start with easy stunts. Work your way up to more difficult stunts. Your coach will let you know when you are ready.

You will hear the words "step, lock, tighten" from your coach often. If you are a flyer, locking your arms and legs while tightening your body helps the bases keep you steady. In addition, bases are often required to lock their knees and elbows.

The *pony mount* is the easiest partner stunt. The base bends her knees slightly. Her feet should be shoulder-width apart. Her arms should be locked with her hands on her thighs above her knees. Her head should be up, and her back should be flat.

The flyer stands behind the base. One hand is on the base's lower back. The other is on the base's shoulder. The flyer needs to hop up on the base's back. It is important for the flyer to keep her knees bent and her feet tucked behind the base's back. Once steady, the flyer should raise her arms into a high V position. To dismount, the flyer hops off the base and stands up straight.

A *thigh stand* is another popular and easy stunt. Two bases are used for a thigh stand. They face forward and lunge toward each other. Their inside legs must be bent, with the knee centered over the foot. Their outside legs should be straight. Their inside feet should overlap, one foot behind the other. The flyer stands between the bases. Once the bases are in the lunge position, the flyer places her hands on the shoulders of both bases. She steps onto the thigh of one base and then the other. Once both her feet are secure, the flyer stands

A pony mount is the easiest partner stunt.

A thigh stand is an easy and popular stunt.

RISKY BUSINESS?

Recent studies have shown that cheerleading can be a dangerous sport. New rules and better training for coaches are aimed at making cheerleading less risky. You need to play a part in preventing injuries by listening carefully to your coaches and following their instructions to the letter. Cheerleaders also need to pay attention to each other and look out for risky situations. Following the rules isn't just a good idea—it can keep you safe.

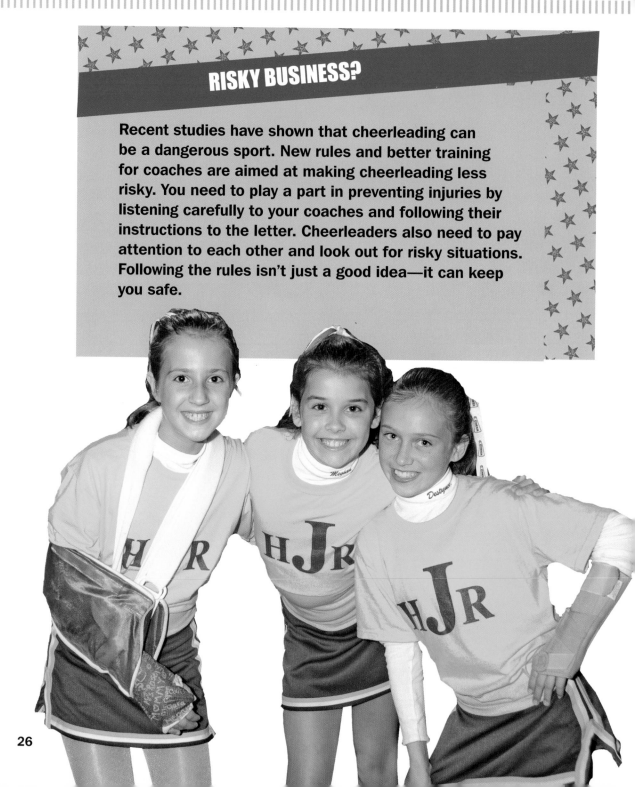

up and moves her hands into a high V position. To help steady the flyer, each base wraps her inside arm around the flyer's leg. Dismounting from a thigh stand is easy. The bases take their outside hands and reach up to grab the flyer's hands. The flyer steps off. Success!

A *shoulder sit* stunt needs only one base. However, until it is performed many times, a back spotter should be used. The base faces forward and lunges to one side. The flyer places her right foot on the base's bent leg close to the hip. The flyer then places her hands on the shoulders of her base, using her base to help her stand. The flyer then stands up on the base's leg, keeping her leg locked and her body tight. She will be standing behind the base, on top of the lunged leg. The base uses her right arm to wrap around the flyer's leg. This helps steady the flyer. The flyer

Flyers keep their muscles taut, with their legs together and arms close to the body.

Cheerleaders for the Indiana Hoosiers perform a shoulder sit.

swings her free leg onto the base's far shoulder. Once her leg is on the base's shoulder, the flyer sits down. The flyer should wrap her legs and feet under the arms of the base. She should now be sitting directly on the base's shoulders. The base will place her hands on the flyer's knees. She will apply slight pressure on the knees so the flyer does not wobble.

To dismount, the flyer needs to unlock her feet from behind the base's back and bring them forward. The base then reaches for the flyer's hands. As she does, she dips down and then pops up, allowing the flyer to jump off. It is important for the base to keep her arms tight in front of her head. The flyer will place much of her body weight onto the hands of her base. When the base dips up and down, the flyer will be popped up enough to be able to bring her legs behind her.

"EVERYONE GETS SCARED, AND EVERYONE FALLS. THE KEY IS TO GET RIGHT BACK UP AND TRY AGAIN."

SHANNON MILLER, OLYMPIC GOLD MEDALIST IN GYMNASTICS

"WHAT MATTERS IS NOT THAT YOU BE THE BEST, BUT THAT YOU TRY YOUR BEST."

She must bring them together again and land on her feet behind the base.

Egypt Wasn't Built in a Day!

After you learn basic stunts, you can put them together to create pyramids. A pyramid is two or more connected stunt groups. The flyers join the pyramids together by linking their hands or legs together.

Some pyramids use every member of the squad.

Cheerleaders in Maryland show off their pyramid style at halftime.

Pyramids are a fun way to up your "wow" factor in routines! Some pyramids use every member of the squad. They are exciting to watch. Your squad will start with easier pyramids and then work up to more difficult ones. To start with the easier pyramids, connect two partner stunts.

NEW SAFETY STANDARDS

As cheer stunting and tumbling grew more popular, the stunts and tumbles became more dangerous. Many people thought they were *too* dangerous. Over the last few years, many new safety regulations have been issued.

For the first time, there are guidelines for elementary, middle school, and junior high cheerleaders. The younger squads needed these guidelines. They were trying to execute skills that were too advanced for them. This often resulted in a lot of falls and injuries.

This means that you will no longer see basket tosses or double full twisting dismounts until the high school level. Also, younger cheer squads must have three catchers when the flyer falls away from the bases to a horizontal flat position. This is much safer than only having two catchers.

There have been recent changes at the high school level, too. Squads are now forbidden to build a pyramid higher than two people.

College rules allow squads to perform pyramids two and a half people high on some surfaces, such as competition mats and football fields.

4
HEAD OVER HEELS: TUMBLING

The crowd goes wild over tumbling! It adds power and pizzazz to routines. The most dynamic cheer routines include tumbling. Sometimes tumbling is used to distract the audience while other cheerleaders set up a stunt. In a cheer routine, someone is always moving. It is usually a tumbler!

Many cheerleaders sign up for tumbling classes at gymnastics centers. This is a great way to start tumbling, because you will have a spotter. These centers have trampolines and cheese mats to help you get started. Learning the proper technique from the very start will help you once you are on a squad, too. Tumbling Coach Ashley Redelico agrees: "There is only one way to become a better tumbler. Like all other sports, you must practice. Make sure

A girl performs on the balance beam. Many cheerleaders hone their tumbling skills in gymnastics classes.

you learn the correct technique from the beginning. Bad habits are hard to break."

Make Your Move

There are four must-have tumbles every cheerleader must be able to do. You have probably done each one hundreds of times in your life so far. But are you doing them the correct way? While they look easy, you do need to practice them with the correct format. Do not go on to more difficult tumbles until you master these.

Handstands are important to tumbling. Many coaches believe that if you perfect your handstand, all of your tumbles will improve. With practice, you will be able to perform a great one!

Stand tall, and lift your hands above your head. Your arms should be straight and touching your ears. Kick your leg in front of you and take a large step forward. Start to lean forward while keeping your body straight. Let your body tip over your lunged leg. Push forward with your lunged leg and

A handstand is one of the basic tumbles all cheerleaders must learn.

back foot. Keep your arms perfectly straight as you approach the ground. Pressure should be on your hands. Push forward or backward with your hands as needed to help straighten yourself. But do not push *too* hard, or you will tumble over!

Forward rolls are easy to do once you learn how. Balance on the balls of your feet in a squat position. Hold your arms out in front of you to help you balance. Put your hands on the floor. Tuck your head in and look down at your stomach. Start to roll forward. Roll slowly onto the back of your

In a backward roll, you start and finish in a squat position.

shoulder region. Always roll on the shoulders to protect your neck and back. Push off with your feet so that your body will roll right over. Keep your legs tucked in as you roll. Push off with your hands and back up onto the balls of your feet. You may have to steady yourself by putting your arms out straight.

Start in a squat position for the *backward roll*. Keep knees and legs together and your back straight. Tuck your chin to your chest. Let your heels drop to the floor. Curl onto

WHAT ARE CHEESE MATS?

A cheese mat, or incline mat, is a cushioned mat that has an incline. It looks like a wedge of cheese. A cheerleader stands on the top (thick) part of the wedge and then practices back handsprings, flips, and tucks. Most cheerleaders need to practice these skills with a cheese mat before they can master them on their own.

your back, and start to roll over. Bend your elbows and point them toward the ceiling. Put your hands on the floor near your head. Push off with your hands and straighten your arms. Your hips will start to lift up as you roll your body over your head. Your feet should return to the floor. Finish in a squat position.

To begin a *cartwheel*, stand in a lunge position and put your right leg in front, knee bent slightly, arms up by your ears. Reach forward with your right arm, kicking your left leg up as you do so. The left hand should follow very quickly, and as it touches the ground, your right leg should be off the ground as well. Your left leg will reach the ground first, followed by the right. You will finish in a lunge, just as you started. This time, the opposite leg will be in front. It may be hard to stay in a straight line while doing a cartwheel.

Cartwheels form the basis for many other stunts.

Try making a line with tape and using it as a guide for your feet and hands. Now that you have learned how to do a cartwheel, round-offs, walkovers, and handsprings should be easier. Why? They all are similar to a cartwheel.

Practicing cartwheels is a no-brainer, according to tumbling Coach Redelico:

A back handspring is a more advanced skill. Beginning cheerleaders should learn cartwheels first.

We all know that spotters are a must when practicing new stunts. But for tumbling, the basics like handstands, cartwheels, and round-offs do not need spotters. You should practice them every day. These simple skills make all other tumbling skills, such as the back handsprings up to full twisting layouts, possible. The basics are valuable and essential. There is no excuse not to nail them.

Once you master the basics, you will learn tumbling passes where you put more than one tumble together. They will involve twists, front passes, and more! You can do *running tumbles.* These tumbles require a running start.

They include cartwheels, round-offs, or other tumbles designed to gain speed so you can do more tumbles. One day you will be good enough to perform an *aerial*. An aerial involves turning completely over in the air without touching the mat with your hands.

Now that you have learned the basics, start practicing your stunts and tumbles—with a spotter when needed, of course! As they say in cheerleading, bring it on! See you on the flip side!

WORDS TO KNOW

aerial—A move in which a cheerleader turns completely over in the air without touching the mat with her hands.

base—A cheerleader at the bottom of a stunt or pyramid. Her feet do not leave the floor. Bases lift the flyer into a stunt.

dismount—A way to return the flyer to the floor after a stunt or mount.

flyer—The cheerleader on the top of a pyramid or stunt. The bases often toss the flyer into the air.

mount—A move in which one or more people are supported in the air by one or more people on the ground. Also referred to as a stunt.

pyramid—Multiple mounts or a group of stunts next to one another. They may or may not be connected.

running tumble—A tumble that requires a running start. They include cartwheels, round-offs, and other tumbles designed to gain speed so that you can do additional tumbles.

spotter—A cheerleader who is responsible for watching the flyer and being prepared to catch her if she falls.

stunting—Any skill involving tumbling, mounting, a pyramid, or toss. Usually does not refer to a jump.

tumbling—A gymnastic skill used in a cheer for crowd appeal. Can be done as an individual or as a group in unison. Some tumbles are back handsprings, back and front tucks, and layouts.

LEARN MORE

BOOKS

Carrier, Justin, and Donna McKay. *Complete Cheerleading.* Champaign, Ill.: Human Kinetics, 2006.

Gruber, Beth. *Cheerleading for Fun.* Minneapolis: Compass Point Books, 2004.

Jones, Jen. *Cheer Basics: Rules to Cheer By.* Mankato, Minn.: Capstone Press, 2006.

Maurer, Tracy Nelson. *Competitive Cheerleading.* Vero Beach, Fla.: Rourke Publishing, 2006.

WEB SITES

American Youth Football and Cheer
   <http://www.americanyouthfootball.com/
      cheerleading.asp>

National Council for Spirit Safety and Education
   <http://www.spiritsafety.com>

Varsity Official Site
   <http://www.varsity.com>

INDEX